World Languages

Families in
French

Daniel Nunn

Chicago, Illinois

Edited by Daniel Nunn, Rebecca Rissman & Sian Smith
Designed by Joanna Hinton-Malivoire
Picture research by Tracy Cummins
Production by Victoria Fitzgerald
Originated by Capstone Global Library Ltd
Printed and bound in China by Leo Paper Products Ltd

16 15 14 13 12
10 9 8 7 6 5 4 3 2 1

Library of Congress Cataloging-in-Publication Data
Nunn, Daniel.
  Families in French : les families / Daniel Nunn.
      p. cm.—(World languages - Families)
  Text in English and French.
  Includes bibliographical references and index.
  ISBN 978-1-4329-7172-4—ISBN 978-1-4329-7179-3 (pbk.) 1. French language—Textbooks for foreign speakers—English—Juvenile literature. 2. Families—Juvenile literature. I. Title.

  PC2129.E5.N86 2013
  448.2'421—dc23   2012020424

Acknowledgments
We would like to thank the following for permission to reproduce photographs: Shutterstock pp.4 (Catalin Petolea), 5 (optimarc), 5, 6 (Petrenko Andriy), 5, 7 (Tyler Olson), 5, 8 (Andrey Shadrin), 9 (Erika Cross), 10 (Alena Brozova), 5, 11 (Maxim Petrichuk), 12 (auremar), 13 (Mika Heittola), 5, 14, 15 (Alexander Raths), 5, 16 (Samuel Borges), 17 (Vitalii Nesterchuk), 18 (pat138241), 19 (Fotokostic), 20 (Cheryl Casey), 21 (spotmatik).

Cover photographs of two women and a man reproduced with permission of Shutterstock (Yuri Arcurs). Cover photograph of a girl reproduced with permission of istockphoto (© Sean Lockes). Back cover photograph of a girl reproduced with permission of Shutterstock (Erika Cross).

We would like to thank Séverine Ribierre for her invaluable help in the preparation of this book.

Contents

Salut!

Je m'appelle Daniel.

Et voici ma famille.

Ma mère et mon père

ma mère

Voici ma mère.

Voici mon père.

Mon frère et ma soeur

mon frère

Voici mon frère.

Voici ma soeur.

Ma belle-mère et
mon beau-père

ma belle-mère

Voici ma belle-mère.

mon beau-père

Voici mon beau-père.

Mon demi-frère et ma demi-soeur

mon demi-frère

Voici mon demi-frère.

ma demi-soeur

Voici ma demi-soeur.

Ma grand-mère et mon grand-père

ma grand-mère

Voici ma grand-mère.

Voici mon grand-père.

Ma tante et mon oncle

ma tante

Voici ma tante.

mon oncle

Voici mon oncle.

Mes cousins

ma cousine

Voici mes cousins.

mon cousin

19

Mes amis

mon amie

Voici mes amis.

Dictionary

French Word	How To Say It	English Word
ami	a-mee	friend (male)
amie	a-mee	friend (female)
amis	a-mee	friends
beau-père	bo-pair	stepfather
belle-mère	bell-mair	stepmother
cousin	koo-zan	cousin (male)
cousine	koo-zeen	cousin (female)
cousins	koo-zan	cousins
demi-frère	de-mee-frair	stepbrother
demi-soeur	de-mee-sir	stepsister
et	ay	and
famille	fa-mee-ya	family
frère	frair	brother
grand-mère	gron-mair	grandmother
grand-père	gron-pair	grandfather
je m'appelle	juh ma-pell	my name is

French Word	How To Say It	English Word
ma	ma	my (female)
mère	mair	mother
mes	may / mez*	my (plural)
mon	mon	my (male)
oncle	on-kle	uncle
père	pair	father
salut	sa-loo	hi
soeur	sir	sister
tante	tont	aunt
voici	vwa-see	this is / these are

* *Mes* is pronounced *mez* when placed before a word beginning with a vowel.

See words in the "How To Say It" columns for a rough guide to pronunciations.

23

Index

Notes for Parents and Teachers

In French, nouns are either masculine or feminine. The word for "my" changes accordingly—either *mon* (masculine) or *ma* (feminine). Sometimes nouns have different spellings too, which is why the word for "cousin" can be spelled either *cousin* (male) or *cousine* (female).

On page 20, the masculine word *mon* is used in the label "mon amie" even though the word *amie* is feminine. This is an exception, and occurs to avoid having the "a" ending of *ma* immediately alongside the "a" sound at the start of *amie*.

ML   10-13